& Sauces & Salsas

&Sauces &Salsas

LOVE FOOD

Love Food ® is an imprint of Parragon Books Ltd

Parragon
Queen Street House
4 Queen Street
Bath BA1 1HE, UK

Copyright © Parragon Books Ltd 2007

Love Food ® and the accompanying heart device is a trademark of Parragon Books Ltd.

Text by Gina Steer
Internal design by Terry Jeavons & Company
Cover design by Luke Griffin
Photographer: Laurie Evans
Home economist: Carol Tennant

ISBN 978-1-4075-6690-0

Printed in China

This book uses imperial, metric, and US cup measurements. Follow the same units of measurement
throughout; do not mix imperial and metric. All spoon measurements are level, unless otherwise stated:
teaspoons are assumed to be 5ml, and tablespoons are assumed to be 15ml. Unless otherwise stated,
milk is assumed to be whole, eggs and individual fruits such as bananas are medium, and pepper is
freshly ground black pepper.

Recipes using raw or very lightly cooked eggs should be avoided by infants, the elderly, pregnant
women, convalescents, and anyone suffering from an illness. Pregnant and breast-feeding women are
advised to avoid eating peanuts and peanut products.

Contents

Introduction

Salsas and sauces were used by ancient civilizations to add flavors and textures to meals, and they have since developed into the delicious mainstays of modern cooking around the world.

Spicy Salsas

In recent times, salsas have become universally popular across many different countries and cultures throughout the world, but they are not a new phenomenon by any means. For centuries, salsas were indigenous to Mexican cooking and were used to add flavor, color, and texture—*salsa* is the Mexican word for "sauce." In fact, references show that they were enjoyed by both the Aztecs and the Mayan civilization.

There are several different varieties of salsa, which include:

- **red salsa (*roje*)**, named after the color of its main ingredient—tomatoes
- **green salsa (*verde*)**, again with reference to its color, which comes from the tomatillo—a small green fruit related to the gooseberry with a papery husk that is discarded
- **cooked salsa (*cocida*)**, in which some or all of the ingredients are cooked or the salsa is added to a dish prior to cooking to impart flavor
- **fresh salsa (*fresco*)**, also called *salsa cruda*, in which, as the name suggests, all the ingredients are fresh and it is served without cooking.

Some salsas are designed to be served with the meal, while others are used in the cooking process. They often take the place of a sauce as well as a salad, providing a healthy accompaniment to any meal. Salsas come in various consistencies, from the smooth-textured that have been processed in a food processor or blender, to the chunky, and can be served cold or hot. However, all salsas are similar in composition, containing vegetables, beans, and in more recent times, fresh or dried fruit, with much of the flavor coming from the addition of chiles and other spices, herbs, seeds, and seasonings. Salsas are usually low in fat.

Basic ingredients routinely used in the making of salsas include:
- **chiles, fresh or dried,** as well as chili powder or dried red chile flakes
- **fresh ripe tomatoes,** which are normally diced, or canned, which are chopped, and tomato paste
- **bell peppers** of all colors, which are usually used in their fresh form, sometimes peeled, but occasionally those preserved in oil are used
- **white and red onions and scallions**, chopped or grated, for imparting texture as well as flavor
- **fresh herbs,** such as cilantro, oregano, and, more recently, basil, flat-leaf parsley, and mint, which are usually finely chopped and added at the end of preparation
- **spices and seeds**, such as cumin and sesame
- **seasonings**, such as freshly ground black or white pepper.

As you will see from the recipes in this book, salsas in all their dazzling variety are simple to prepare. But care must be taken to choose ingredients that are as fresh as possible and of good quality to ensure maximum flavor and appeal.

Special Sauces

The use of sauces, including gravies, has been traced back as far as Roman times (*c.* AD 200), brought about by the need to mask the taste of tainted food. Without the benefits of refrigeration, fish and seafood, poultry and meats quickly deteriorated, especially in hot weather, so sauces and gravies were developed as an effective way to make the food more palatable. Both sauces and gravies were highly flavored with herbs or spices and had a coating or pouring consistency to help improve the appearance of the finished dish. In earlier times, bread was often used as the thickening agent; it was only much more recently that the French devised the butter and flour paste, or *roux*, and egg yolk and cream or oil liaison. In fact, it is the French who are credited with introducing the term *sauce* to describe a liquid designed to improve the look and taste of a dish, and they developed many of the classic varieties, including the five main sauces, known as "mother sauces," from which all the classic sauces are derived: Béchamel, Espagnole, Hollandaise, Tomato, and Velouté.

Béchamel

This is one of the great white sauces, flavored with onion, mace, carrot, peppercorns, and bay leaf, originally used to disguise any rancid taste from the milk in the days before refrigeration. Sometimes water was used in place of milk for the same reason. There are a few theories as to the sauce's origin, but the most likely is that the chef François Pierre de La Varenne at Louis XIV's court in the 17th century invented it, along with other "mother sauces." He is credited with devising haute cuisine and wrote *Le Cuisinier François* (The True French Cooking), in which Béchamel Sauce was included.

Espagnole

This a a brown roux sauce that chef Francois Pierre de La Varenne did not include in his *Le Cuisinier François*, although he featured a very similar sauce instead—Sauce Robert. The first mention of Espagnole Sauce was not until the 18th century, but it quickly established itself as one of the "mother sauces."

Hollandaise

This sauce is reputed to have been devised by either the Flemish or Dutch and named after where the creamy butter used to make it originally came from. Many believe that it was taken from Holland to France by the Huguenots in the 17th century.

Tomato

It is thought that the very first tomato sauces came from South America and were in fact salsas. Tomatoes were introduced to Europe in the 16th century when explorers brought them back from their expeditions. It is hard to believe today that the tomato was treated with suspicion at first. It was during the 18th century in America that the popularity of tomato sauce really began to grow. Teaming so successfully with rice and pasta, it was adopted by both Spain and Italy and by the 20th century had become used by most cuisines around the world.

Velouté

This is a white sauce made using a roux and white stock—chicken or veal. It forms the base of many other sauces, among them being Allemand, a sauce that uses an egg yolk and cream liaison to thicken it. Other sauces included in this category are Supreme Sauce, which is served with chicken dishes, and Vin Blanc Sauce—a fish velouté made with shallots, herbs, and butter.

Mayonnaise

Antonin Carême, a celebrated French chef, is one of the many to whom the development of this hugely popular sauce is attributed. It was originally called *mahonnaise*, but it became "mayonnaise" simply through a misspelling in a cookbook published in 1841.

These great classic sauces, as well as others from around the globe, all featured in this book, will quickly transform everyday ingredients into dishes with distinction.

Spicy Salsas

Any one of the salsas in this enticingly varied collection will add color, flavor, and texture to a wide range of dishes, for everyday eating and entertaining. Fresh (uncooked) salsas include a classic Tomato Salsa, fragrant with cilantro, and a chunky, citrusy Avocado Salsa, together with some refreshing yet creamy yogurt-based salsas. For a touch of warmth and excitement, try Warm Tomatillo Salsa, laced with tequila, and Roasted Corn Salsa, flavored with fresh chiles and mint. You can also sample some exotic specialties from around the world, including Jamaican Salsa vibrant with guavas and banana from the West Indies, Asian Peach Salsa redolent with peaches and perfumed star anise from the Far East, or Turkish Salsa enriched with pomegranate, figs, and honey.

Tomato Salsa

**4 ripe tomatoes,
about 8 oz/225 g total weight**

1 small red onion

1 fresh red jalapeño chile, seeded

1–2 garlic cloves, crushed

2-inch/5-cm piece cucumber

1 tsp (or to taste) honey

1 tbsp chopped fresh cilantro

pepper

Makes about 1 cup

1 Seed the tomatoes, finely chop, and put in a small nonmetallic bowl. Finely chop the onion and chile and add to the tomatoes with the garlic.

2 Peel the cucumber with a swivel-bladed vegetable peeler. Cut in half and scoop out and discard the seeds. Finely chop the flesh and add to the bowl with the honey and pepper to taste.

3 Add the cilantro and stir well. Lightly cover and let stand in a cool place, but not the refrigerator, for 30 minutes to let the flavors develop.

TASTY TIP
This versatile fresh salsa can be served with any meats, poultry, or fish and seafood, but is perfect with tortilla chips. To ensure a really great tasting salsa, make sure that you choose fully ripe tomatoes and that all the ingredients are finely chopped.

Avocado Salsa

**2 ripe tomatoes,
about 4 oz/115 g total weight**

2 ripe avocados

**3 tbsp freshly squeezed
lime juice**

6 scallions

2–3 garlic cloves, crushed

**1 fresh red serrano chile,
seeded and finely chopped**

1 celery stalk, finely chopped

**3 tbsp drained canned red
kidney beans, rinsed, drained,
and coarsely chopped**

1 tsp honey

**1 tbsp chopped
fresh cilantro**

pepper

Makes about 2 cups

1 Make a cross in the stalk end of each tomato, put in a heatproof bowl, and pour over boiling water to cover. Let stand for 2 minutes, then remove with a slotted spoon and let cool. When cool enough to handle, peel away the skins. Cut into quarters, seed, and finely chop.

2 Cut the avocados in half and remove and discard the pits. Peel, then finely chop the flesh and put in a separate bowl. Pour over the lime juice and gently stir until the avocados are thoroughly coated in the lime juice. Stir in the chopped tomatoes.

3 Finely chop the scallions and add to the bowl with the garlic, chile, and celery. Add the beans to the bowl with the honey, pepper to taste, and cilantro. Stir well, then transfer to a nonmetallic serving bowl, lightly cover, and let stand in a cool place, but not the refrigerator, for 30 minutes to let the flavors develop.

TASTY TIP
A zingy salsa, ideal as an accompaniment to a steaming bowl of chili con carne or any other Mexican-style dishes. Or serve it as a dip with tortilla chips. You can also replace the finely chopped avocado with mashed avocado, then add all the remaining ingredients.

Three Bean Salsa

2 oz/55 g fresh or frozen
fava beans

2 oz/55 g green beans,
coarsely chopped

2 tbsp olive oil

2 shallots, finely chopped

1–3 garlic cloves, crushed

1 fresh red serrano chile,
seeded and finely chopped

3 tbsp drained red kidney
beans, rinsed, drained,
and coarsely chopped

2 tomatoes, about 4 oz/115 g,
coarsely chopped

2 tbsp canned pickled chiles,
drained and finely chopped

1 tsp (or to taste) honey

1 tbsp chopped fresh cilantro

Makes about 1 cups

1 Cook the fava beans with the green beans in a pan of boiling water for 4–5 minutes until tender. Drain well.

2 Heat the oil in a small heavy-bottomed pan, add the shallots, garlic, and fresh chile and gently sauté, stirring frequently, for 5 minutes.

3 Add the cooked green beans with the kidney beans, tomatoes, pickled chiles, and honey. Heat over medium heat, stirring occasionally, for 5–8 minutes until thoroughly heated through. Stir in the cilantro and serve warm.

TASTY TIP
Full of enticing color, flavor, and texture, this lively salsa makes an interesting filling for crisp taco shells, or serve with any poultry or meats, such as lamb steaks or kabobs. This is a chunky salsa, but you can process it in a food processor or blender if a smoother salsa is preferred.

Roasted Corn Salsa

2 corncobs

1 tbsp unsalted butter, melted

4 garlic cloves, crushed

2 fresh red serrano chiles,
seeded and finely chopped

4 oz/115 g broccoli, blanched and
finely chopped into tiny florets

1 red onion, finely chopped

2 ripe tomatoes, about 4 oz/115 g,
peeled and finely chopped

1 tsp (or to taste) white
wine vinegar

1–2 tsp maple syrup

1 tbsp chopped fresh mint

Makes about 2 cups

1 Preheat the oven to 350°F/180°C. Remove and discard the outer leaves and silky threads from the corncobs and lightly rinse. Put each cob on a 6-inch/15-cm square of foil.

2 Lightly brush each cob with the melted butter, then sprinkle over the garlic and chiles. Lift the sides of each foil square up and fold over at the top to encase the cobs, transfer to a roasting pan, and roast in the preheated oven for 20–30 minutes until tender. Remove from the oven and let cool.

3 When the cobs are cool enough to handle, strip off the kernels with a knife and put in a small bowl. Add all the remaining ingredients and stir well. Lightly cover and let stand in a cool place, but not the refrigerator, for 30 minutes to let the flavors develop.

4 Gently reheat, stirring occasionally, for 5–8 minutes and then serve warm.

TASTY TIP
You can use this deliciously chunky and sweet, warm salsa to pep up any dish, such as vegetable or meat enchiladas or fajitas. It also makes an eye-catching addition to any barbecue spread and is a great accompaniment to charbroiled fish steaks, such as tuna.

Herb Salsa

3-inch/7.5-cm piece cucumber

2 tsp salt

6 scallions, finely chopped

2 celery stalks, finely chopped

1 green bell pepper, peeled,
seeded, and finely chopped

⅔ cup lowfat plain
or strained plain yogurt

1 tbsp shredded fresh basil

1 tbsp chopped fresh
flat-leaf parsley

1 tbsp chopped fresh oregano

Makes about 1½ cups

1 Peel the cucumber very thinly and cut lengthwise into quarters. Scoop out and discard the seeds. Finely chop the flesh, put in a nonmetallic strainer, and sprinkle with the salt. Let drain for 15–20 minutes, then rinse thoroughly and drain well. Put in a small bowl.

2 Add the scallions, celery, and green bell pepper to the bowl and mix well. Add the yogurt and stir well before adding all the herbs. Stir again, then spoon into a serving dish. Lightly cover and let stand in a cool place, but not the refrigerator, for 30 minutes to let the flavors develop.

TASTY TIP
Full of fresh, fragrant flavor from three types of herbs, this healthful salsa would complement salmon steaks well in both color and taste, or try it as an accompaniment to Middle Eastern-style roasted eggplants. You can use other combinations of herbs—try fresh marjoram, parsley, and chives, for instance.

Chile and Garlic Salsa

4 garlic cloves

1–3 fresh red serrano chiles

1–2 oz/25–55 g pickled chiles,
drained and finely chopped

1 large zucchini, about
6 oz/175 g, grated

1 large carrot, about 6 oz/175 g,
peeled and grated

2 tsp soy sauce

1 tsp honey

1 tbsp chopped fresh cilantro

Makes about 1½ cups

1 Finely crush the garlic and put in a small bowl. Cut the fresh chiles in half, remove and discard the seeds and membranes, and finely chop. Alternatively, if a hotter salsa is preferred, leave the seeds and membranes in place and finely chop. Add to the garlic with the pickled chiles.

2 Stir the zucchini and carrot with the soy sauce and honey into the bowl. Add the cilantro and stir well.

3 Transfer the salsa to a small pan and gently heat, stirring occasionally, for 3–5 minutes before serving.

TASTY TIP
This carrot- and zucchini-based, chile-spiked salsa packs a powerful punch, so serve with robust-tasting meat dishes, such as pork steaks or kabobs or beef steaks. If you have a high heat tolerance, increase the amount of either the fresh or pickled chiles.

Yogurt Salsa

3-inch/7.5-cm piece cucumber

1 tsp salt

4 scallions, finely chopped

**1 zucchini, about
4 oz/115 g, grated**

**1 red bell pepper, seeded
and finely chopped**

1¼ cups strained plain yogurt

**1 tbsp chopped fresh
flat-leaf parsley**

**1–2 tsp (or to taste)
chili powder**

pepper

Makes about 1½ cups

1 Cut the cucumber lengthwise into quarters. Scoop out and discard the seeds. Coarsely grate the flesh, put in a nonmetallic strainer, and sprinkle with the salt. Let drain for 15–20 minutes, then rinse thoroughly and drain well. Put in a small bowl.

2 Add the scallions, zucchini, and red bell pepper to the bowl and mix well. Add the yogurt and parsley with the chili powder and pepper to taste. Stir well, then spoon into a serving dish. Lightly cover and let stand in a cool place, but not the refrigerator, for at least 30 minutes to let the flavors develop.

TASTY TIP
This Middle Eastern-inspired creamy salsa goes perfectly with any lamb dish, such as koftas, meatballs, steaks, or kabobs. The salsa can also be used to spice up a variety of seafood dishes, and is an excellent accompaniment to sea bass or crab, for example.

Lowfat Yogurt Salsa

scant ⅓ cup dried apricots

1¼ cups lowfat plain or strained plain yogurt

3 tbsp rolled oats

1–2 tsp (or to taste) honey

1 fresh green jalapeño chile, seeded and finely chopped

6 scallions, finely chopped

1 carrot, about 4 oz/115 g, peeled and grated

2 tbsp chopped fresh mint

few dashes of Hot Pepper Sauce sauce, to taste

pepper

Makes generous 1½ cups

1 Finely chop the apricots and put in a small bowl. Add the yogurt with the rolled oats and honey.

2 Stir well, then add the chile, scallions, carrot, and mint with pepper to taste. Stir again, then add the Hot Pepper Sauce.

3 Spoon into a serving bowl. Lightly cover and let stand in a cool place, but not the refrigerator, for at least 30 minutes to let the flavors develop. Store in the refrigerator if keeping for longer.

TASTY TIP
Give yourself a healthy treat with this sweet, aromatic, creamy salsa—a great accompaniment to corncobs, or broiled, grilled, or barbecued Mediterranean vegetables. If the salsa is served too cold, the flavor will be impaired. If keeping for more than 1 hour before serving, remove from the refrigerator 30 minutes before serving.

Warm Tomatillo Salsa

1 small red bell pepper

1 small green bell pepper

1–2 (or to taste) fresh
red jalapeño chiles

1 tbsp olive oil

2–3 garlic cloves, crushed

2 shallots, finely chopped

8 oz/225 g tomatillos

1 tbsp chopped fresh cilantro

2 tsp maple syrup

1 tbsp (or to taste) tequila

pepper

Makes about 2 cup

1 Preheat the broiler to high and line the broiler rack with foil. Cut the red and green bell peppers into quarters and remove and discard the seeds and membranes. Put on the foil-lined broiler rack with the chile. Cook under the preheated broiler for 10 minutes, or until the skins are charred and blistered, turning the chile occasionally.

2 Remove from the heat, transfer to a plastic bag, and let cool for 10 minutes. Peel away the skins from the bell peppers. Peel away the skin from the chile, cut in half, and remove and discard the seeds and membrane. Finely chop the bell peppers and chile.

3 Heat the oil in a heavy-bottomed pan, add the garlic and shallots, and gently sauté, stirring frequently, for 5 minutes. Add the chopped bell peppers and chile.

4 Cut the tomatillos into quarters and finely chop the flesh. Add to the pan with the remaining ingredients. Heat gently, stirring occasionally, for 5–8 minutes until thoroughly heated through. Serve warm.

TASTY TIP
Citrusy, fragrant-tasting tomatillos make a wonderful base for a salsa, with the addition of tequila providing an extra kick here. Serve Tex-Mex-style to add zing to a dish of beef or vegetable fajitas, or to spice up plain broiled beef steaks.

Caribbean Salsa

1 small ripe mango, peeled

1 small ripe papaya, peeled

1–2 (or to taste) fresh
habanero chiles

4 scallions, finely chopped

1–2 tsp maple syrup

½ small fresh coconut

1 tbsp chopped fresh cilantro

pepper

Makes about 1½ cups

1 Remove and discard the pit from the mango. Finely chop the flesh and put in a bowl. Scoop out and discard the seeds from the papaya. Finely chop the flesh and add to the mango.

2 Cut the chile in half, remove and discard the seeds and membrane, and finely chop. Add to the fruit with the scallions and maple syrup.

3 Discard any outer shell from the coconut, leaving the white coconut flesh. Grate the coconut flesh. Add to the fruit with the cilantro and pepper to taste. Spoon into a serving dish. Lightly cover and let stand in a cool place, but not the refrigerator, for at least 30 minutes to let the flavors develop.

TASTY TIP
This recipe brings together the perfect combination of sweet and vibrant mango and delicate papaya with fresh coconut to make this exotic-tasting salsa. It is an excellent way to add color and flavor to grilled or barbecued swordfish steaks or kabobs.

Jamaican Salsa

**generous ⅛ cup drained
canned corn kernels**

**1 large ripe banana
finely grated**

rind of 1 lime

**2 tbsp freshly squeezed
lime juice**

**2 ripe guavas, about 4 oz/115 g
total weight**

**1–2 fresh Jamaican hot chiles,
seeded and finely chopped**

**1 small red onion,
finely chopped**

1 tsp (or to taste) honey

1¼ cups plain yogurt

1 tbsp chopped fresh cilantro

pepper

Makes about 1½ cups

1 Cook the corn kernels in a pan of boiling water for 3–4 minutes until tender. Drain well.

2 Peel the banana and mash in a nonmetallic bowl. Add the lime rind and juice, then gently stir until the banana is thoroughly coated in the lime juice. Stir in the corn kernels.

3 Peel the guavas, seed, and finely chop the flesh. Add to the bowl with the chile, onion, and honey.

4 Stir in the yogurt with the cilantro and pepper to taste. Stir well, then spoon into a serving bowl. Lightly cover and let stand in a cool place, but not the refrigerator, for at least 30 minutes to let the flavors develop.

TASTY TIP
Bring an inviting taste of the West Indies to your summer barbecue or alfresco meal with this sumptuous banana and guava-flavored salsa, with a chile-hot edge—ideal with chicken wings or drumsticks. If liked, add some grated fresh coconut and a little rum to give the salsa a kick.

Creole Pineapple Salsa

3-inch/7.5-cm piece cucumber

1 tsp salt

½ small ripe fresh pineapple,
about 4 oz/115 g peeled
and cored weight

6 scallions, chopped

1 fresh red Anaheim chile,
seeded and finely chopped

1–2 tsp Hot Pepper Sauce

1–2 tsp maple syrup

1 tbsp chopped fresh mint

generous ⅛ cup unsalted
cashews, coarsely chopped

Makes about 1 cup

1 Peel the cucumber with a swivel-bladed vegetable peeler and cut lengthwise into quarters. Scoop out and discard the seeds. Finely chop the flesh, put in a nonmetallic strainer, and sprinkle with the salt. Let drain for 15–20 minutes, then rinse thoroughly and drain well. Put in a bowl.

2 Discard any outer skin from the pineapple and cut away and discard any central core. Either finely chop the flesh with a large cook's knife or put in a food processor and process for 1 minute, or until finely chopped. Add to the cucumber with the scallions and chile.

3 Add the Hot Pepper Sauce with the maple syrup and mint. Spoon into a serving dish. Lightly cover and let stand in a cool place, but not the refrigerator, for at least 30 minutes to let the flavors develop. Sprinkle with the cashews just before serving.

TASTY TIP
Hot, fruity, sweet, and crunchy, this is a sensational salsa for a dish of broiled or barbecued shrimp, or served with cold cooked seafood as a cocktail-style appetizer. You can also use canned pineapple instead of fresh, draining thoroughly before chopping.

Asian Peach Salsa

3 ripe peaches

1–2 fresh Thai chiles

2 lemongrass stalks

1-inch/2.5-cm piece
fresh ginger root

2 tsp sesame oil

1 whole star anise

2 tsp soy sauce

1 tbsp honey

1 small bok choy, about
1 oz/25 g, finely shredded

1 tbsp sesame seeds

Makes about 2 cups

1 Make a cross in the top of each peach, put in a large heatproof bowl, and pour over boiling water to cover. Let stand for 1–2 minutes, then remove with a slotted spoon and let cool. When cool enough to handle, peel away the skins. Cut in half, remove and discard the pits, and finely chop the flesh.

2 Cut the chile in half, remove and discard the seeds and membrane, and finely chop. Remove and discard the outer leaves of the lemongrass stalks and lightly bruise with a mallet or rolling pin. Cut into small pieces. Peel the ginger and finely grate.

3 Heat a wok for 30 seconds over high heat. Add the oil, swirl around to coat the bottom of the wok, and heat for 30 seconds. Add the chile, ginger, lemongrass, and star anise and stir-fry for 1 minute. Add the peaches with the soy sauce, honey, and bok choy and stir-fry for 2 minutes. Spoon the salsa into a bowl.

4 Lightly cover and let stand in a cool place, but not the refrigerator, for 30 minutes to let the flavors develop. Carefully remove the lemongrass pieces and star anise. Sprinkle with the sesame seeds and serve.

TASTY TIP
Full of fragrant flavors provided by lemongrass, ginger, and star anise, this fruity salsa also delivers a hit of chile. Serve with crispy duck or Peking duck, or pan-fried duck breasts. Nectarines or fresh apricots can be used in place of the peaches. If using apricots, use about 8 oz/225 g fresh fruit.

Tropical Salsa

1 small wedge watermelon, about 4 oz/115 g

2 blood oranges, if available, or 1 red grapefruit

1–2 fresh green jalapeño chiles

2 tsp honey

2 oz/55 g preserved ginger, drained and 2–3 tsp syrup from the jar reserved

1 tbsp chopped fresh mint

Makes about 1½ cups

1 Peel the watermelon, seed, and finely chop. Put in a bowl. Working over the bowl to catch the juices, peel the oranges, removing and discarding all the bitter white pith. Separate into segments, chop the flesh, and add to the watermelon.

2 Cut the chile in half, remove and discard the seeds and membrane, and finely chop. Add to fruit with the honey. Stir well.

3 Finely chop the preserved ginger and add to the bowl with the ginger syrup. Add the mint and stir well. Transfer the salsa to a serving bowl. Lightly cover and let stand in a cool place, but not the refrigerator, for 30 minutes to let the flavors develop. Stir again and serve.

TASTY TIP
This salsa is a treat for both the eye and the taste buds, featuring colorful watermelon and blood orange flavored with sweet and aromatic preserved ginger. It teams especially well with any poultry dish, such as turkey or chicken kabobs.

Apple and Habanero Chile Salsa

1 small orange bell pepper

1 small green bell pepper

1 green apple

2 tbsp freshly squeezed lemon juice

1–2 (or to taste) fresh habanero chiles

6 scallions, finely chopped

1 tbsp maple syrup

2–3 tsp (or to taste) Hot Pepper Sauce

1 tbsp chopped fresh mint

Makes about 2 cups

1 Preheat the broiler and line the broiler rack with foil. Cut the orange and green bell peppers into quarters and remove and discard the seeds and membranes. Put on the foil-lined broiler rack and cook under the preheated broiler for 10 minutes, or until the skins are charred and blistered.

2 Remove from the heat, transfer to a plastic bag, and let cool for 10 minutes. Peel away the skins and finely chop the flesh.

3 Cut the apple into quarters and cut away and discard the core. Coarsely grate the flesh and put in a bowl. Pour over the lemon juice and stir well until the apple is thoroughly coated in the lemon juice. Add the bell peppers.

4 Cut the chile in half, remove and discard the seeds and membrane, and finely chop. Add to the apple and peppers with all the remaining ingredients. Stir well and spoon into a nonmetallic serving dish. Lightly cover and let stand in a cool place, but not the refrigerator, for at least 30 minutes to let the flavors develop. Stir again and serve.

TASTY TIP
Transform a dish of pork chops or steaks with this fiery yet fruity salsa. If you don't like your salsa too hot, then you can easily moderate the heat level according to your taste. If habanero chiles are unavailable, try using a Scotch bonnet or Thai chile.

Turkish Salsa

1–2 (or to taste) fresh red
jalapeño chiles

4 scallions, finely chopped

2 oranges

1 ripe pomegranate

2 ripe figs

2 tsp honey

1 tbsp snipped fresh chives

1 tsp toasted cumin seeds

Makes about 1 cup

1 Cut the chile in half, remove and discard the seeds and
membrane, and finely chop. Put in a bowl with the scallions.

2 Working over the bowl to catch the juices, peel the oranges,
removing and discarding all the bitter white pith. Separate into
segments, finely chop the flesh, and add to the chile and scallions.

3 Cut the pomegranate in half and scoop out the seeds. Add
them to the orange mixture. Lightly rinse the figs and finely chop.

4 Add the chopped figs to the bowl with the honey and chives.
Stir well and spoon into a nonmetallic serving dish. Lightly
cover and let stand in a cool place, but not the refrigerator, for
30 minutes to let the flavors develop. Sprinkle with the cumin
seeds and serve.

TASTY TIP
This delightfully different salsa is perfect with
broiled or barbecued lamb. Try it with skewers
threaded with cubes of cheese and baguette
browned under the broiler or on the barbecue.
To toast cumin seeds, put in a nonstick skillet
and gently heat, stirring, for 3–4 minutes until
you smell the spice, and let cool before using.

Tex-Mex Salsa

1 large avocado

2 tbsp freshly squeezed
lime juice

1 white onion, coarsely grated

1–3 (or to taste) fresh green
jalapeño chiles

1–2 tsp maple syrup

2 oz/55 g drained canned pinto
beans, rinsed and drained

8 oz/225 g ripe tomatoes,
peeled if preferred

1 tbsp chopped fresh cilantro

Makes about 1¾ cups

1 Cut the avocado in half and remove and discard the pit. Peel, then finely chop the flesh. Put in a bowl. Pour over the lime juice and gently stir until the avocado is thoroughly coated in the lime juice. Stir in the onion.

2 Cut the chile in half and remove and discard the seeds and membrane. Finely chop the flesh. Add to the avocado with the maple syrup.

3 Coarsely chop the pinto beans and add to the bowl. Cut the tomatoes into quarters, seed, and finely chop the flesh. Add to the bowl with the cilantro.

4 Stir the salsa well and spoon into a nonmetallic serving dish. Lightly cover and let stand in a cool place, but not the refrigerator, for 30 minutes to let the flavors develop.

TASTY TIP
This pretty salsa makes a great accompaniment to Tex-Mex-style meat, poultry, or fish dishes, or simply serve with nachos or tortilla chips. If keeping for more than 30 minutes, to prevent the avocado from turning brown, put the avocado pit in the center of the salsa. Remove before serving.

Mexican Salsa

1–2 (or to taste) dried
ancho chiles

1–2 (or to taste) fresh
red serrano chiles

1–2 (or to taste) fresh
green serrano chiles

1 zucchini, about 4 oz/115 g

4 ripe tomatoes, about
8 oz/225 g total weight

2 tsp maple syrup

1 tbsp freshly squeezed lime juice

1 tbsp chopped fresh cilantro

Makes about 1 cup

1 Put the dried chile in a heatproof bowl, cover with almost boiling water, and let soak for 20 minutes. Drain well and then finely chop.

2 Cut the fresh chiles in half and remove and discard the seeds and membranes. Finely chop the flesh and put in a bowl with the chopped dried chile.

3 Coarsely grate the zucchini and add to the chiles. Cut the tomatoes into quarters, seed, and finely chop the flesh. Add to the chiles with the remaining ingredients. Stir well and spoon into a nonmetallic serving dish. Lightly cover and let stand in a cool place, but not the refrigerator, for 30 minutes to let the flavors develop. Stir again and serve.

TASTY TIP
This delicious recipe provides an unadulterated blast of old Mexico, searingly hot with chile, tangy with lime, and fragrant with fresh cilantro. The salsa is particularly good with any Mexican dish, such as chicken, beef, or vegetable fajitas or enchiladas.

Special Sauces

Sauces are quickly and easily prepared, yet can enhance the flavor and appearance of a dish immeasurably and turn simple ingredients into memorable meals. Clear and concise recipes are given here for the five key "mother sauces," together with variations on the main methods to provide a range of serving ideas. There are also recipes for flavorful stocks, together with some classic accompaniments such as Cranberry Sauce and Mint Sauce, as well as some speedy and delicious pasta sauces, such as Fresh Tomato Sauce, and the ever-popular Pesto made from fresh basil. The chapter also features the favorite sauces of other international cuisines—Mexican Green Sauce and the powerful chocolate-flavored Mole Sauce, Chinese pungent Black Bean Sauce, and Indonesian and Malaysian creamy, nutty Satay Sauce.

Brown Stock

2 lb/900 g meat bones, raw or cooked

1 large onion, chopped

1 large carrot, chopped

2 celery stalks, chopped

1 Bouquet Garni

7¼ cups water

Makes about 5 cups

1 Preheat the oven to 400°F/200°C. Put the bones in a roasting pan and roast in the preheated oven for 20 minutes, or until browned. Remove from the oven and let cool.

2 Chop the bones into small pieces and put in a large pan with all the remaining ingredients. Bring to a boil, then reduce the heat, cover, and simmer for 2 hours.

3 Strain and leave until cold, then remove all traces of fat. Store covered in the refrigerator for up to 4 days. Boil vigorously for 5 minutes before using. The stock can be frozen into ice-cube trays for up to 1 month.

TASTY TIP
For a fresh Bouquet Garni, place 1 piece of celery, 1–2 small pieces celery stalk, 2–3 cloves, 1 bay leaf, few black peppercorns, 2–3 fresh parsley sprigs, and 1 fresh thyme sprig in the center of a small piece of cheesecloth, then tie up with a long length of clean string, which can then be tied to the pan handle for easy removal.

Béchamel Sauce

1¼ cups milk

1 small onion

2–3 cloves

1 mace blade

1 fresh bay leaf

3–4 white peppercorns, if available, or black peppercorns

1 small piece carrot, peeled

2 tbsp unsalted butter or margarine

scant ¼ cup all-purpose flour

1 tbsp light cream (optional)

salt and pepper

Makes about 1½ cups

1 Pour the milk into a small heavy-bottomed pan with a lid. Stud the onion with the cloves and add to the milk with the mace, bay leaf, peppercorns, and carrot. Heat over gentle heat and slowly bring to just boiling point. Remove from the heat, cover, and leave for at least 30 minutes for the flavors to infuse. When ready to use, strain and reheat until warm.

2 Melt the butter in a separate small pan and sprinkle in the flour. Cook over gentle heat, stirring constantly with a wooden spoon, for 2 minutes.

3 Remove from the heat and gradually stir in the warmed infused milk, adding a little at a time and stirring constantly until the milk is incorporated before adding more. When all the milk has been added, return to the heat and cook, stirring until thick, smooth, and glossy. Add salt and pepper to taste and cream, if using, then use as required.

TASTY TIP
This is the spice-enhanced version of the standard white sauce, with a pouring consistency. It can be served with all kinds of meat, poultry, and fish, but is especially good with ham, and is also ideal as a topping for stuffed cannelloni and for enriching lasagna.

Espagnole Sauce

**1 bacon slice,
preferably unsmoked**

2 tbsp unsalted butter

1 shallot, finely chopped

1 small carrot, diced

2 tbsp all-purpose flour

1¼ cups Brown Stock, warmed

1–2 tsp tomato paste

salt and pepper

Makes about 1 cup

1 Remove and discard the rind and any cartilage from the bacon and chop. Melt the butter in a small heavy-bottomed pan, add the bacon, and sauté for 1 minute. Add the shallot and carrot and sauté, stirring frequently, for an additional 3–4 minutes until the butter is lightly brown (take care that it does not burn).

2 Remove from the heat, sprinkle in the flour, and stir well. Return to the heat and cook, stirring constantly, for 2 minutes. Remove from the heat and gradually stir in the stock.

3 Return to the heat and cook, stirring constantly, until the sauce has thickened. Reduce the heat to a very gentle simmer and cook for 40–45 minutes, stirring frequently and checking that the sauce is not sticking on the bottom. Strain the sauce, skimming off any fat, and add salt and pepper to taste, together with the tomato paste.

TASTY TIP
For a Demi-glace Sauce, make a Gravy by draining the fat from a roasting pan used to cook a meat joint, then gently heat the remaining sediment with 1¼ cups of hot vegetable stock. Add seasoning to taste and cook, stirring for 3–5 minutes. Stir in an equal quantity of Espagnole Sauce, add seasoning and 1 teaspoon unsalted butter and heat until the butter has melted.

Hollandaise Sauce

2 tbsp white wine vinegar

1 tbsp water

2 egg yolks

6–8 tbsp unsalted butter, slightly softened and diced

lemon juice (optional)

salt and pepper

Makes about 1 cup

1 Pour the vinegar and water into a small heavy-bottomed pan and bring to a boil. Boil for 3 minutes, or until reduced by half. Remove from the heat and let cool slightly.

2 Put the egg yolks in a heatproof bowl and beat in the cooled vinegar water. Set over a pan of gently simmering water, ensuring that the bottom of the bowl does not touch the simmering water.

3 Cook, stirring constantly with a wooden spoon, until the mixture thickens slightly and lightly coats the back of the spoon.

4 Keeping the water simmering, add the butter, a piece at a time, until the sauce is thick, smooth, and glossy. Add a little lemon juice if the mixture is too thick and to give a more piquant flavor. Add salt and pepper to taste and serve warm.

TASTY TIP
Mayonnaise is a versatile variation. Beat an egg yolk, ½ teaspoon mustard powder, ½–1 teaspoon superfine sugar, and seasoning in a bowl until creamy. Then add about ⅔ cup extra virgin olive oil, drop by drop, beating well with a balloon whisk. Add 1 tablespoon white wine vinegar gradually. Store in the refrigerator up to 2 days.

Velouté Sauce

2 tbsp unsalted butter

2 tbsp all-purpose flour

1½ cups Chicken Stock, warmed

2–3 tbsp light cream

1–2 tbsp freshly squeezed
lemon juice

salt and pepper

Makes about 1½ cups

1 Heat the butter in a small heavy-bottomed pan until melted, then sprinkle in the flour. Cook over gentle heat, stirring constantly with a wooden spoon, for 2 minutes.

2 Remove from the heat and gradually stir in the warmed stock, stirring thoroughly after each addition. When all the stock has been added, return to the heat and cook, stirring constantly, until the sauce is reduced slightly, has thickened, and lightly coats the back of the spoon.

3 Remove from the heat and stir in the cream with the lemon juice and salt and pepper to taste. Serve warm.

TASTY TIP
To make the Chicken Stock, place 1 chicken carcass (broken into pieces), 1 Bouquet Garni, 1 small onion (halved), 1 small chopped carrot, 1 small celery stalk, 1 mace blade, and 7¼ cups water into a large pan. Bring to a boil, then reduce the heat, cover, and simmer for 2 hours. Strain and boil vigorously for 5 minutes before using.

Barbecue Sauce

1 tbsp olive oil

1 small onion, finely chopped

2–3 garlic cloves, crushed

1 fresh red jalapeño chile, seeded
and finely chopped (optional)

2 tsp tomato paste

1 tsp (or to taste) mustard powder

1 tbsp Worcestershire sauce

1 tbsp red wine vinegar

2–3 tsp dark brown sugar

1¼ cups water

Makes about 1 cup

1 Heat the oil in a small heavy-bottomed pan, add the onion, garlic, and chile, if using, and gently sauté, stirring frequently, for 3 minutes, or until beginning to soften. Remove from the heat.

2 Blend the tomato paste with the mustard powder, Worcestershire sauce, and vinegar to a paste, then stir into the onion mixture with 2 teaspoons sugar. Mix well, then gradually stir in the water.

3 Return to the heat and bring to a boil, stirring frequently. Reduce the heat and gently simmer, stirring occasionally, for 15 minutes. Check the sweetness and add the remaining sugar, if liked. Strain, if preferred, and serve hot or let cool and serve cold.

TASTY TIP
The perfect accompaniment to barbecued meat or poultry, this sauce can also be used as a marinade for brushing over the food as it cooks on the barbecue. But take care that it doesn't burn. For barbecued vegetables or fish, such as salmon, or other oily fish, use white wine vinegar and light brown sugar, and omit the garlic.

Beurre Blanc

2 tbsp finely chopped shallot

2 tbsp white wine vinegar

8 tbsp unsalted butter

salt and pepper

Makes about ½ cup

1 Put the shallot in a small heavy-bottomed pan with the vinegar and salt and pepper to taste. Bring to a boil and boil for 2–3 minutes until reduced to about 2 teaspoons.

2 Add 2 tablespoons of the butter and beat vigorously with a wire whisk while bringing to a boil. Remove from the heat and whisk in the remaining butter, a piece at a time. When all the butter has been added, check and adjust the seasoning if necessary and serve.

TASTY TIP
This wonderfully refined and classic sauce is excellent when served with any white fish, but it is especially delicious with trout fillets. The sauce is also a perfect accompaniment to eggs, vegetables, and poultry. Note that the consistency of the Beurre Blanc should be slightly thinner than Mayonnaise.

Red Wine Sauce

⅔ cup Gravy or Espagnole Sauce

4 tbsp red wine,
such as a Burgundy

1 tbsp red currant preserve

Makes about 1 cup

1 Blend the Gravy with the wine and pour into a small heavy-bottomed pan. Add the red currant preserve and heat over gentle heat, stirring, until blended.

2 Bring to a boil, then reduce the heat and simmer for 2 minutes. Serve hot.

TASTY TIP
This simple, but richly colored and flavored, sauce is ideal for anointing roast beef or lamb. It is also a perfect addition to any rich meat dish, such as venison, pheasant, or partridge. Make sure that you make enough of this delicious sauce to go round.

Cranberry Sauce

1 lb/450 g fresh or thawed
frozen cranberries

1 tbsp grated orange rind,
preferably unwaxed organic

⅔ cup freshly squeezed orange
juice, preferably organic

scant ½–generous ½ cup
(or to taste) light brown sugar

⅔ cup water

1–2 tbsp Cointreau (optional)

Makes about 2 cups

1 Put the cranberries in a heavy-bottomed pan with the orange rind and juice, scant ½ cup sugar, and water. Bring to a boil, then reduce the heat and simmer for 12–15 minutes until the cranberries have burst.

2 Remove from the heat, check the sweetness, and add the remaining sugar, if liked, with the Cointreau, if using. Serve warm or cold.

TASTY TIP
This sharp-tasting sauce goes well with roasted poultry, such as turkey, and game. It can also be served as a condiment with cold cooked meats and strong-flavored cheese. Add 2–4 cloves and 1–2 whole star anise to give an aromatic flavor. Replace the orange juice with red wine and add a little port at the end of cooking.

Mint Sauce

3 tbsp chopped fresh mint

2–3 tsp (or to taste) superfine sugar

2 tbsp just-boiled water

3–4 tbsp white wine or malt vinegar

Makes about ½ cup

1 Put the mint in a small heatproof bowl and add 2 teaspoons sugar. Let the boiled water cool for about 1 minute, then pour over the mint. Stir until the sugar has dissolved, then let infuse for 10 minutes.

2 Add the vinegar to taste, cover, and let stand for 1 hour. Stir and serve.

TASTY TIP
This classic sweet herb sauce goes perfectly with roast lamb, but it can also be served with broiled or pan-fried lamb steaks or chops. Try adding a spoonful to a lamb casserole. For a richer flavor, replace 1 tablespoon white wine vinegar with balsamic vinegar.

Apple Sauce

about 5 large tart cooking apples,
about 2 lb/900 g total weight

generous ½ cup superfine sugar

2–3 tbsp water

2 tbsp unsalted butter

Makes about 2 cups

1 Peel, core, and chop the apples. Put in a heavy-bottomed pan with the sugar and water. Bring to a boil, then reduce the heat, cover, and simmer, stirring occasionally, for 10–12 minutes until the apples have collapsed and are fluffy.

2 Add the butter and stir until melted. Beat with a wooden spoon until smooth. Serve warm or cold.

TASTY TIP
The sauce can also be flavored with other ingredients to suit the dish it is to be served with, such as: 1–2 tablespoons grated lemon or orange rind; 3–4 cloves or 1–2 whole star anise (remove before serving); 1 lightly bruised cinnamon stick (remove before serving), or 1 teaspoon ground cinnamon.

Tapenade

1¼ cups pitted black olives

⅓ cup capers, drained

1 tbsp chopped fresh thyme

2 garlic cloves

1 tsp Dijon mustard

2 oz/55 g canned anchovy fillets

⅔ cup virgin olive oil

about 2 tbsp brandy

1 tbsp chopped fresh
flat-leaf parsley

pepper

Makes about 2 cups

1 Put the olives, capers, thyme, garlic, and mustard in a food processor and process for 1 minute. Add the anchovy fillets with their oil and process for an additional 2–3 minutes until a thick paste is formed.

2 With the motor running, slowly pour in the oil in a thin, steady stream until a thick sauce is formed.

3 Scrape into a bowl and stir in enough brandy to give a thick sauce. Add pepper to taste and stir in the parsley. Spoon into a small serving bowl and serve.

TASTY TIP
Originating from Provence in France, this piquant paste is traditionally served as an accompaniment to fish or meat dishes, such as tuna steaks, but is equally delicious spread on toast triangles or thick slices of toasted baguette, or as a dip for crudités.

Fresh Tomato Sauce

1 tbsp olive oil

1 small onion, chopped

2–3 garlic cloves,
crushed (optional)

1 small celery stalk,
finely chopped

1 bay leaf

1 lb/450 g ripe tomatoes,
peeled (optional) and chopped

1 tbsp tomato paste,
blended with ⅔ cup water

few fresh oregano,
thyme, or basil sprigs

pepper

Makes about 4 cups

1 Heat the oil in a heavy-bottomed pan, add the onion, garlic, if using, celery, and bay leaf, and gently sauté, stirring frequently, for 5 minutes.

2 Stir in the tomatoes with the blended tomato paste. Add pepper to taste and the herb sprigs. Bring to a boil, then reduce the heat, cover, and simmer, stirring occasionally, for 20–25 minutes until the tomatoes have completely collapsed. If liked, simmer for an additional 20 minutes to give a thicker sauce.

3 Discard the bay leaf and other herbs. Transfer to a food processor or blender and process to a chunky purée. If a smooth sauce is preferred, rub through a fine nonmetallic strainer. Taste and adjust the seasoning if necessary. Reheat until hot and use as required.

TASTY TIP
To make Provençal sauce, add 1 small peeled, seeded, and chopped red and yellow bell pepper and a small diced zucchini to the prepared sauce. Simmer until the peppers and zucchini are tender. Stir in 2 tablespoons chopped pitted olives and 1 tablespoon shredded fresh basil. Heat until hot.

Arrabiata Sauce

2 tbsp olive oil

2 garlic cloves, chopped

1 fresh red serrano chile,
seeded and chopped

1 tbsp grated lemon rind

1 lb/450 g ripe tomatoes,
peeled and chopped

1 tbsp tomato paste,
blended with ⅔ cup water

pinch of superfine sugar

1 tbsp balsamic vinegar

1 tbsp chopped fresh marjoram

pepper

Makes about 2½ cups

1 Heat the oil in a heavy-bottomed pan, add the garlic and chile, and sauté, stirring, constantly, for 1 minute. Sprinkle in the lemon rind and stir, then add the tomatoes with the blended tomato paste. Add the sugar and bring to a boil, then reduce heat and simmer for 12 minutes.

2 Add the vinegar and marjoram and simmer for an additional 5 minutes. Add pepper to taste. Serve hot.

TASTY TIP
Serve this tangy chile-hot tomato sauce with pasta shapes, such as penne, or spaghetti. Unlike many other tomato sauce and pasta dishes, it is not traditionally served with grated Parmesan cheese. Crushed dried red chiles can be used in place of the fresh chile and fresh flat-leaf parsley in place of the marjoram.

Pesto

2 oz/55 g fresh basil leaves

1 garlic clove

generous ⅛ cup toasted pine nuts

6 tbsp extra virgin olive oil

2 tbsp freshly grated
Parmesan cheese

1–2 tsp freshly squeezed
lemon juice (optional)

salt and pepper

Makes about 1 cup

1 Tear the basil leaves coarsely into pieces and put in a large mortar with the garlic, pine nuts, and 1 tablespoon of the oil. Pound with a pestle to form a paste.

2 Gradually work in the remaining oil to form a thick sauce. Add salt and pepper to taste and stir in the Parmesan cheese. If liked, slacken slightly with the lemon juice.

3 Alternatively, put the basil leaves with the pine nuts and a little of the oil in a food processor and process for 1 minute. Scrape down the sides of the bowl. With the motor running, gradually add the remaining oil in a thin, steady stream.

4 Scrape into a bowl, then stir in pepper to taste and the Parmesan cheese. If liked, slacken with the lemon juice.

TASTY TIP
Serve with linguine, spaghetti, gnocchi, or with a soup. Use watercress or arugula in place of the basil leaves. You can also replace the basil leaves with fresh cilantro leaves and add 1 tablespoon chopped fresh chile. Peeled roasted bell peppers can be added to the basil leaves when pounding.

Chipotle Sauce

2–4 dried chipotle chiles

2 tbsp olive oil

4 bacon slices, chopped

1 large onion, finely chopped

2–3 garlic cloves, crushed

2 celery stalks, finely chopped

2 tbsp tomato paste

⅔ cup stout, such as Guinness

⅔ cup Vegetable or Brown Stock

2 tbsp dark brown sugar

1 tsp prepared English mustard

1–2 tsp Worcestershire sauce

2 tbsp chopped fresh cilantro

pepper

Makes about 2½ cups

1 Put the chiles in a heatproof bowl, pour over hot water to cover, and soak for 30 minutes, or until softened. Drain, reserving the soaking liquid, and finely chop the chiles.

2 Heat the oil in a heavy-bottomed pan, add the bacon, onion, garlic, and celery, and sauté, stirring frequently, for 15 minutes. Blend the tomato paste with the reserved soaking liquid and stir into the pan, then add the chiles, stout, and stock. Add the sugar with the mustard and Worcestershire sauce, stir well, and bring to a boil.

3 Reduce the heat, cover, and simmer, stirring occasionally, for 30 minutes. Add pepper to taste and stir in the cilantro. Use as required.

TASTY TIP
To make the Vegetable Stock, put 1 large onion, cut into wedges, 2 chopped carrots, 1 chopped celery stalk, 1 Bouquet Garni, and generous 6½ cups water in a large pan, and bring to a boil. Reduce the heat, cover, and simmer for 40 minutes, then strain. Store in the refrigerator for up to 3 days. Boil vigorously for 5 minutes before using.

Mexican Green Sauce

1 lb/450 g fresh green
Anaheim chiles

1 large onion, quartered

3 garlic cloves

2 tbsp olive oil

1¼ cups Vegetable Stock

2 tbsp chopped fresh cilantro

salt and pepper

Makes scant 2 cups

1 Preheat the broiler to high and line the broiler rack with foil. Thinly slice 1 chile and reserve for garnishing. Put the remaining chiles on the foil-lined broiler rack and cook under the preheated broiler for 10 minutes, or until the skins are charred and blistered. Remove from the heat, transfer to a plastic bag, and let cool for 10 minutes.

2 Meanwhile, put the onion and garlic on the foil-lined broiler rack, drizzle with 1 tablespoon of the oil, and cook under the broiler for 5–8 minutes until softened. Alternatively, sauté the onion and garlic in the oil in a skillet.

3 Peel away the skins of the whole chiles. Put in a food processor with the onion and garlic and process for 1 minute. With the motor running, slowly pour in the remaining oil in a thin, steady stream, and then the stock, to form a chunky sauce.

4 Scrape into a bowl, add salt and pepper to taste, and stir in the cilantro. Serve warm, sprinkled with the sliced chile.

TASTY TIP
A vibrant, fiery sauce for serving with all manner of Mexican favorites, such as enchiladas, chimichangas, or empanadas, or with broiled or grilled salmon, swordfish steaks, or kabobs. Other chiles can be used in place of Anaheim chiles. Choose ones with a medium heat rating.

Mole Sauce

3 dried ancho chiles

3 dried pasillo chiles

3 dried mulatto chiles

1 onion, sliced

2–3 garlic cloves, crushed

scant ⅛ cup sesame seeds

generous ⅛ cup toasted
almonds, cut into slivers

1 tsp ground coriander

4 cloves

½ tsp pepper

2–3 tbsp sunflower oil

1¼ cups Chicken or
Vegetable Stock

1 lb/450 g ripe tomatoes,
peeled and chopped

2 tsp ground cinnamon

scant ⅓ cup raisins

scant ½ cup pumpkin seeds

2 oz/55 g good-quality
dark chocolate

1 tbsp red wine vinegar

Makes about 3 cups

1 Put all the chiles in a heatproof bowl, pour over very hot water to cover, and let soak for 30 minutes.

2 Drain the chiles, put in a food processor with the onion, garlic, sesame seeds, almonds, coriander, cloves, and pepper and process to form a thick paste. Alternatively, pound in a large mortar with a pestle.

3 Heat the oil in a heavy-bottomed pan, add the paste, and sauté, stirring frequently, for 5 minutes. Add the stock with the tomatoes, cinnamon, raisins, and pumpkin seeds. Bring to a boil, then reduce the heat and simmer, stirring occasionally, for 15 minutes, or until reduced by about half and thickened.

4 Break the chocolate into small pieces and add to the sauce with the vinegar. Cook gently for 5 minutes, then use as required.

TASTY TIP
This classic Mexican sauce, enriched with dark chocolate, is usually served with chicken. Try it with broiled, grilled, or barbecued chicken breasts, or simmer chunks of chicken in the sauce. You can also add 1 tablespoon unsweetened cocoa when making the paste in Step 2, if liked.

Creole Sauce

2 tbsp sunflower oil

1 red bell pepper,
seeded and thinly sliced

1 green bell pepper,
seeded and thinly sliced

1 onion, thinly sliced

2–3 garlic cloves, crushed

1 fresh red chile,
seeded and chopped

1 tsp ground coriander

1 tsp ground cumin

1 lb/450 g ripe tomatoes,
peeled and chopped

1¼ cups Vegetable Stock

4 oz/115 g okra,
trimmed and chopped

1 tbsp chopped fresh cilantro

salt and pepper

Makes about 3½ cups

1 Heat the oil in a heavy-bottomed pan, add the bell peppers, onion, garlic, and chile, and sauté, stirring frequently, for 3 minutes. Add the ground coriander and cumin and sauté, stirring frequently, for an additional 3 minutes.

2 Stir in the tomatoes and stock and bring to a boil. Reduce the heat and simmer, stirring occasionally, for 15 minutes, or until the sauce has reduced slightly.

3 Add the okra to the pan with salt and pepper to taste and simmer for an additional 10–15 minutes, or until the sauce has thickened. Stir in the fresh cilantro and use as required.

TASTY TIP
Enjoy a taste of the Deep South with this vibrant, spicy sauce, the chopped okra lending it both characteristic flavor and thickness. Serve with cooked shrimp and long-grain rice for a gumbo-type dish. If okra is unavailable, thicken the sauce with 1 tablespoon cornstarch blended to a paste with 2 tablespoons water.

Teriyaki Sauce

**1-inch/2.5-cm piece
fresh ginger root**

**1¼ cups shoyu
(Japanese soy sauce)**

**3 tbsp white wine
or cider vinegar**

**3 tbsp mirin
(sweet rice wine)**

2–3 tbsp superfine sugar

Makes about 1 cup

1 Peel and grate the ginger. Put in a small heavy-bottomed pan with the shoyu, vinegar, mirin, and 2 tablespoons sugar.

2 Gently heat, stirring, until the sugar has dissolved. Check the sweetness and add the remaining sugar, if liked, heating gently, stirring, until the sugar has dissolved.

3 Boil the mixture for 5–8 minutes, or until reduced by half. Remove from the heat. If wanting to use immediately, stand in a bowl of ice and water for 30 minutes, or until cool. Alternatively, leave until cool, then use as required.

TASTY TIP
This famous Japanese sauce is a perfect dipping sauce for cooked chicken, salmon, or shrimp. It can also be used for brushing over kabobs before broiling or barbecuing or for marinating fish, chicken, beef, or pork. Once cold, strain, pour into a sterilized bottle or jar, and store in the refrigerator for up to 2 weeks.

Black Bean Sauce

1 tbsp peanut oil

2 tbsp fermented black beans, finely chopped

1 garlic clove, chopped

1 tbsp grated fresh ginger root

1 shallot, chopped

2 scallions, finely chopped

2 small fresh green chiles, seeded and chopped

1 tbsp light soy sauce

1 tbsp strained freshly squeezed lemon juice

⅔ cup Vegetable Stock

1–2 tsp (or to taste) superfine sugar

salt and pepper

Makes about ⅔ cup

1 Heat a wok over high heat for 30 seconds. Add the oil, swirl around to coat the bottom of the wok, and heat for 30 seconds. Add the black beans, garlic, ginger, and shallot and stir-fry for 2 minutes.

2 Add the scallions and chiles and stir-fry for 3 minutes. Add the soy sauce and lemon juice and simmer for 2 minutes. Add the stock and sugar with salt and pepper to taste and simmer for an additional 2 minutes. Use as required.

TASTY TIP
Fermented black beans, sometimes called Chinese black beans, have a uniquely salty, pungent flavor that marries particularly well with stir-fried beef. If storing the Black Bean Sauce, leave until cold, then pour into a sterilized bottle or jar and store in the refrigerator for up to 2 weeks.

Satay Sauce

1 shallot, chopped

1–2 garlic cloves, chopped

1–2 fresh jalapeño chiles, seeded and chopped

1-inch/2.5-cm piece fresh ginger root, peeled and grated

1½ tsp ground turmeric

2 tsp light brown sugar

2 tbsp white wine vinegar

1 tbsp light soy sauce

1 tbsp freshly squeezed lemon juice

2 tbsp peanut oil

1¼ cups coconut milk

¾ cup roasted unsalted peanuts

Makes about 1¼ cups

1 Put the shallot, garlic, chile, and ginger in a mortar and pound to a paste with a pestle. Alternatively, use a small food processor. Add the turmeric and continue to pound or process until the paste is well blended.

2 Stir in the sugar, vinegar, soy sauce, lemon juice, oil, and coconut milk and stir until well blended.

3 If necessary, rinse the food processor and thoroughly dry, then finely chop the peanuts in the processor. Stir into the coconut milk mixture.

4 Pour into a heavy-bottomed pan and bring to a boil. Reduce the heat and simmer, stirring frequently, for 10 minutes. Remove from the heat and let cool. Use as required. Store covered in the refrigerator for up to 3–4 days.

TASTY TIP
This Indonesian peanut-based favorite can be served with small beef, lamb, pork, chicken, or shrimp skewers as a delicious appetizer. The sauce can also be used as a marinade. Coat foods with the satay mixture, cover, and let marinate in the refrigerator for at least 30 minutes.

Index